I was on LInkedIn the other day, chatting with a fellow Veteran. After 20 years of active duty service, he had recently transitioned to civilian life and was looking for a job.

"I've sent out 500 resumes and I've got two interviews," he said.

Because it was via chat on LinkedIn, I couldn't tell if he was bemoaning the lack of return on his efforts or if he was excited because he got two interviews.

My thoughts were, **TWO INTERVIEWS!**

> *How long must it have taken to find 500 companies with a job opening, research each one and tweak the resume to sound at least a little customized for the job?*

To get *TWO* **INTERVIEWS!**

And THAT is what motivated me to write this eBook.

2023 Prosperity Franchise Group

This book is dedicated to MY WHY,

My husband John and our
3 awesome kids, ...
Mallory, James and Brendan.

They are the reason I chose franchise ownership. It provided the time and path to financial freedom to be present for them.

As a Vet, I know the skills you learned in the military. I know the character you have; you wouldn't have made it through bootcamp without it. Above all, I know your commitment to getting the job done. So why in the world would you give your expertise to someone else so they make money? So they control your future? So they dictate which days you can take off or what hours of each day you work? Worst of all, so they can limit your financial success?

F**K the Resume

There are 200,000 military personnel who transition to civilian life every year.

? How many of those were in your MOS that may be applying for the same job?

? How many civilians are applying for it?

? How many people who already work for the company are requesting a lateral move or a promotion to the position?

The odds are stacked against you, just by virtue of the numbers.

No wonder job hunting is so stressful, demoralizing and exhausting.

Add to that, there isn't even a person reading the resumes on the other end. Yes you read that right. People don't read resumes anymore. Artificial Intelligence does.

You have to have the right keywords that match what the company is looking for *and* you have to use each keyword frequently enough that the Artificial Intelligence that is scanning the resume documents it.

This is such a challenge these days that there are companies built around helping you write your resume so Artificial Intelligence doesn't filter you out.

Even reputable job sites like recruiter.com offer advice on what your resume should say. "When reading a resume, **AI looks for technical skills, soft skills, experience, dates, locations, and personal information**. Common sense says the more often you list a certain skill on your resume, the higher the weight the AI will assign to that particular skill."

Common sense? It's nonsense!

When I got out ...

When I got out of the Marine Corps I worked for a very, very short time in the mortgage industry as a loan processor. I quickly realized I knew what I was doing, I could figure out how to put a loan package together and then I said, "I want to be a loan officer." I was connecting with home buyers and my client base was realtors and I really enjoyed helping people buy their dream house.

Yet, that was a very stressful time in the mortgage industry.

The economy was healthy, interest rates were half of what they were a decade earlier and lenders became lax in qualifying buyers.

In the early 2000s, the economy was strong, interest rates were low and consumers felt a bit flush – all of which helped push real-estate values up across the country. With values escalating, lenders felt more confident about making mortgages to customers whose poor credit histories had prevented them from buying homes in the past.

The theory was, when values are rising, borrowers are less likely to default, because they can take money out of their homes if they run into trouble.

The moment of my epiphany

My husband and I were on an anniversary weekend in Scottsdale, Az in 2005. He booked a massage for me at the resort spa. It was called Spaterre or Spaterra, something like that.

I went down for my massage and in the middle of the massage I started sobbing. The massage therapist thought she'd hurt me. I said, "nope" I just had an epiphany. [Side note - that's when Oprah was helping people discover their Ah-ha moments.]

Still sobbing, I went back to the hotel room and told my hubby that I booked a couples massage for the next day. Back in '05, a couple's massage cost over $400. So not cheap.

I needed him to have the experience of what I was talking about.

I wasn't allowed to bring my laptop on vacation. The point of the vacation was to de-stress because I needed to decompress from the pressure of the mortgage business.

We went in for a massage and afterwards I said to myself and my husband, "I need to find out more about massage and I need more massage in my life." My mom had arthritis in her back and I knew she would benefit from massage therapy as well.

I couldn't wait to get back to my computer to research the massage industry.

At first my mindset was, "I could do this cheaper." But the more research I did, the more I came to realize that building a business from scratch is enormously complicated.

Something as simple as choosing the wrong location can be the difference between success and failure.

What's Your Next Career?

When you enter civilian life, you have Five Options

1. Get a civilian job
2. Get a civil service job
3. Start your own company
4. Buy a franchise
5. Retire for life (or for a while and then choose from the other four options.)

25% of veterans say they want to own their own business

"Own your own business" can mean either a business you build from scratch or buying a franchise. In both scenarios, you own your own business. But there are several important differences.

Start a business from scratch

☑ You'll need a product or service to sell.

☑ You'll need to do market research prior to opening to ensure there's a need or desire for your product/service.

☑ You'll most likely need a loan. Most banks don't loan money for an independent start up because it isn't a proven entity.

☑ How are your marketing skills? You'll need to either do it yourself or pay someone to do it.

☑ If you're opening a brick and mortar business, you'll need a commercial real estate agent and an architect.

☑ Are you familiar with the software for Customer Relationship Management, Lead Generation, Lead Nurturing, Accounting, Bookkeeping, Scheduling? You'll need it.

☑ Do you have a mentor, a support team and someone to turn to when you need help? You'll want them. You'll need them.

Buy a Franchise

By comparison, buying and running a franchise is simple.

Franchising is very similar to home ownership. You'll need to have some skin in the game (like a down payment on a house.)

Franchisors want to know you've got skin in the game, but you don't have to finance the whole deal yourself.

The Small Business Administration loan program is known for its competitive terms, low interest rates and 2500 franchise brands that they've already deemed worthy of financing. Of course, *you* still need to qualify for a loan, but the franchise is "pre-approved".

The franchisor also wants to know that you've got some skill you can bring to the table, which of course you do. Whether it's your analytical skills, technical skills, project management skills, collaboration skills, productivity skills, it doesn't matter. Unlike applying for a job where each position is looking for a specific skill set.

There are so many franchise options, we will match a business opportunity with your skills rather than you trying to find the needle in the haystack where your skills match their job opening.

Instead of you sending out 500 resumes for two potential opportunities, how about you have 500 opportunities and you select two to consider?

That's how the franchise industry works.

But, like the house-buying analogy, there are a few steps before this.

1. First you decide what state you want to live in.
2. Then you decide what city you want to live in.
3. Then you decide what community you want to live in.
4. Then you decide what street you want to live on.
5. THEN you select the house. For whatever reason. Family's there. You love the weather. Whatever your reason is.

It's also like dating. You're dating the franchisor. And guess what? Your intro call is your FIRST DATE!

? Do I like them?
? Do they appear honest?
? Do they have integrity?
? Can I see myself enjoying their company for the next 5, 10 or 20 years?

Trust your gut. If you don't like them, move on. There are 4,000 franchise brands. Or as my Dad used to say, "There's plenty of fish in the sea!"

Buying a Franchise - The Process

Though the process of buying a franchise isn't complicated, it is a series of steps that really need to be completed in the correct order. Just like a military process. You know how this works. This is in your wheelhouse, your comfort zone.

Pre-qualification Phase

1 **Getting Started**
We start with a self-evaluation which helps you identify your strengths, goals, and areas of opportunity. It also allows us to establish a clear background, so we can provide the highest level of Franchisor support where needed.

2 **Financial Qualifications**
After the self-evaluation phase, we move into assessing financial qualifications. By asking you to fill out a financial form, we can understand your net worth and identify investment opportunities that fit within your budget. Remember, there is financing available but the bank and the Franchisor will both expect you to contribute some of your own money.

It's important to know the total required investment is to get your franchised business up and running.

This number will include your franchise fee, your opening inventory, the cost of all your furniture, fixtures, and equipment (FF&E), legal fees, and up to 12 months of working capital. Understanding all the start-up expenses including the amount of working capital needed before you are cash flowing is important.

Rule of thumb: you'll need a minimum of **$50k** cash injection.

In the event you need a loan to fund your new business, we have several referral partners that provide a variety of funding options, including SBA financing, ROBS, (Rollover for business, start-ups).

SIDE NOTE: There are 650 franchises listed with the International Franchise Association that offer incentives and discounts for veterans and their spouses.

Brand Exploration Phase

③ Researching Industries

The first step in this phase is narrowing down the 34+ industries to a handful of industries to research.

While some people's inclination is to jump into the "hot" industries, which we can identify for you, that's not always the best move. It's like buying trendy clothes; they don't often stay in fashion long enough to justify the investment. Instead, we recommend you strongly consider the "steady eddie" industries which consistently perform while often remaining under the radar.

Another consideration is what type of business is needed in your community. Is there really a need for *one more coffee shop?*

④ Identifying Industry And Brands

Once you've researched the industries, select one or two and then it's time to drill down to specific brands that match your vision, mission, and values while taking into consideration both your financial resources and your investment goals.

While many so-called "experts" will tell you to follow your passion, I don't agree. You don't have to love fitness to open your own fitness franchise. Nor do you have to do all the work.

Many businesses thrive when they are run by a manager who is responsible for selling your products or services. This will allow you to grow and scale your franchised business by working "on your business not in your business".

You'll also want to fully consider whether you want a business that is open Monday-Friday (maybe Saturdays) like a home service business, or would you be comfortable with a business that is open 7-days a week, like the food service industry?

Do you want to be a passive, semi-absentee owner, or do you want to work in your business?

How well do they align with your business and lifestyle goals?

What is their online reputation? Like it or not, social media is here to stay. When one location of a company gets slammed online, every location feels the hit. Google the name of the franchise + reviews and see what customers are saying. Not that this is the be-all, end-all but you want to consider the customers' overall opinions of the business.

Conversely, avoid lists of "best" franchises. These lists are often click-bait for the media or website who wrote it. Or it's a "pay-to-play" list where franchisors buy an ad and get a listing. Most importantly, it doesn't matter what anyone else thinks is the "best" franchise. The best franchise for you is the one that fits your goals, lifestyle and budget.

Here's a perfect example.

Indeed is a job site. How do they know what the best franchises are? The criteria for inclusion in their list was "the ease of starting the business and the support available to franchisees."

What does "ease of starting the business" even mean? Did they survey existing franchisees to determine the amount of support available?

indeed   Find jobs   Company reviews   Find salaries

Career Guide   Finding a job   Resumes & cover letters ▾   Interviewing   Pay & salary   Career development ▾

Career development > 45 Best Franchises To Own In 2022

45 Best Franchises To Own In 2022

By Indeed Editorial Team
January 13, 2022

Are you ready to be your own boss? Buying a franchise is a great way to start a business. Owning a franchise allows you to get started quickly due to brand recognition and resources provided by the parent company. Exploring different franchising opportunities can help you compare and decide which investment is right for you. In this article, we provide a list that features 45 of the best franchise opportunities of 2022 across a variety of categories. We also offer tips for evaluating franchise opportunities and how to know if you're ready to become a franchisee.

⑤ Meeting With Franchisor

This is where it starts to feel real. Once you've identified your preferred brand(s), you or your franchise consultant will set up a meeting between you and the Franchisor where you'll discuss the business in more detail. This allows the Franchisor to vet you and you to vet them. The Franchisor will be interested in:

☑ **Your Financial Situation** This is important for them because they want you to be successful. They don't want you to fail due to lack of working capital.

☑ **Educational History** This will be more important to certain Franchisors than others, depending on the industry or service.

☑ **Previous Employment** Franchisors love veterans because they know that veterans have learned to strive for flawless execution of plans while in the military. In the Franchise industry, successfully executing the Franchisor's plan is the fastest way to success.

☑ **Motivation for Buying** Franchisors want you to be enthusiastic about their brand. They also want you to articulate how you see your experience, education, personal and professional experience being a fit for their business. In other words, they want to feel that you want to be a part of their community. As was mentioned earlier, this is like a first date.

☑ Demonstrate a clear understanding of responsibilities

The Franchisor wants to know that you understand the requirements of a Franchisee.

Bottom line, the Franchisor needs to be assured that you can seamlessly invest and operate the franchise. We will be sure you're prepared to WOW them so they want you even more than you want them.

But you don't want to just listen to what the Franchisor has to say. You'll also want to talk with current Franchisees. And not just the successful ones. Talk with vintage owners and newer owners. We'll provide you with the recommended questions to ask. Here are a few of the questions, to give you an idea:

? What were the keys to success?

? What were some of the challenges, and how'd they overcome them?

? If they were starting today, knowing what they know now, what would they do differently?

? Does the franchisor provide ongoing support?

? Were there any closures or any transfers? If so, why?

If you feel awkward about asking these questions; don't. It is common practice in the franchise industry. Plus the other Franchisees will become your new Corps, so this is your chance to see if you like them; if you can see yourself among them.

6 **Franchise Disclosure Document (FDD) Review**
If all goes well through the interview and the franchisor identifies you as a good fit, they will send you a copy of their Franchise Disclosure Document (FDD).

This is the regulatory document that the Federal Trade Commission requires Franchisors to provide prospective Franchisees as part of the pre-sale process. The FDD is a legal document that outlines how the business relationship between the franchisee and franchisor will be conducted. For a detailed overview of the FDD, please see Attachment 1.

We strongly recommend you review the FDD with a franchise attorney as this document is very specific to the franchise industry.

7 **Discovery Days**
Some Franchisors may call it something different, but it's still the same across all Franchises. Discovery Day is your opportunity to meet the leadership team and learn more about the franchise: its business processes, brand, and profitability.

Final Phase

⑧ Validation Process

We are aware of how finances can affect a sale, thus, we are here to help you identify the best funding opportunities. To simplify the process for you, we connect you to a group of industry partners (lenders and bankers) who can best match your financial needs.

⑨ Franchise Awarded

At the end of this process, you'll be awarded the license to start building your own business.

Congratulations!
You are a business owner.

Whether you're creating a secondary income stream or parlaying your earnings into additional opportunities to grow, scale, and diversify investments, you are now on your way to creating Legacy Wealth.

Veterans in Franchising

66,000 FRANCHISE BUSINESSES IN U.S. OWNED BY VETERANS

1 IN 7 FRANCHISES IS OWNED BY A VETERAN

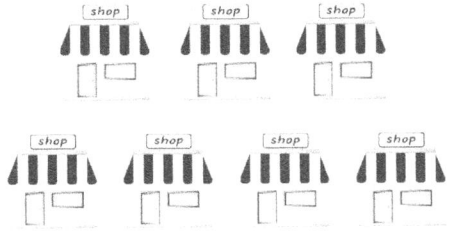

VET—OWNED FRANCHISES EMPLOY 815,000 PEOPLE

VET—OWNED FRANCHISE BUSINESSES GENERATE $41 BILLION IN GDP

What is a Franchise Disclosure Document used for?

This document allows franchisees to make an educated decision about the franchise system before entering into a business relationship. Potential franchisees must enter into this agreement with their eyes open, fully aware of what they are getting involved in.

When should a Franchisee receive a Franchise Disclosure Document?

The Federal Franchise Rule states that the FDD must be disclosed to a potential franchisee no less than 14 days prior to them signing a franchise agreement or paying any money to the franchisor. Once the prospective franchisee signs the FDD receipt page (item 23 of the document), the 14-day period begins.

When do you sign a franchise disclosure document?

Signing the FDD does not signify an agreement to buy a franchise. Rather, it begins the 14-day clock during which the potential franchisee can review the document and determine if they would like to engage in more serious talks about purchasing a business.

Summary of the FDD items

Item 1: The Franchisor and Any Parents, Predecessors, and Affiliates: A description of the company and its history.
Item 2: Business Experience: Business experience including the biographical and professional information of all franchisors and its officers, directors, and executives.
Item 3: Litigation: Information regarding current and past criminal and civil litigation for the franchisor and its management.
Item 4: Bankruptcy: Information regarding the franchisor and any management who have gone through bankruptcy.
Item 5: Initial Fees: The initial fees franchisees will incur in addition to the range and factors that determine the sum of those fees.

Item 6: Other Fees: A description of any other fees or payments that must be made.

Item 7: Estimated Initial Investment: The initial investment in table format and includes all expenditures required by the franchisee to establish the business.

Item 8: Restrictions on Sources of Products and Services: The restrictions that the franchisor has established regarding the source of products or services.

Item 9: Franchisee's Obligations: The franchisor must disclose the franchisee's obligations under the franchise agreement. This is presented as a reference table and includes a summary of all legal obligations to include (but not limited to) site selection, opening obligations, and any obligations upon termination of the franchise agreement.

Item 10: Financing: Whether or not the franchisor offers financing arrangements and, if so, what the terms and conditions of those arrangements are.

Item 11: Assistance, Advertising, Computer Systems, Training: The services that the franchisor will provide to the franchisee.

Item 12: Territory: This item requires the franchisor to disclose if the franchisee will be awarded a protected territory, how that territory will be determined, and any instances when the franchisor may operate with the franchisees' territory.

Item 13: Trademarks: The franchisor must disclose any trademarks within the franchise system. This includes whether they are registered with the United States Patent and Trademark Office, their registration status, and whether there have been any notices of a trademark dispute or conflict.

Item 14: Patents, Copyrights, and Proprietary Information: This section dictates how the franchisee may use any patents and copyrights.

Item 15: Obligation to Participate in the Actual Operation of the Franchise Business: This item explains the obligations that the individual franchisee owner must have in the day-to-day operations of the business. This includes whether they must work in the franchised business full time.

Item 16: Restrictions on What the Franchisee May Sell: The franchisor must disclose what control they have over what can be sold as part of the franchised business.

Item 17: Renewal, Termination, Transfer, and Dispute Resolution: A disclosure and summary of the legal rights and obligations in regards to renewal and terminations and what the franchisee's rights and restrictions are during a disagreement with the franchisor.

Item 18: Public Figures: Disclosure of any public figures (celebrities or public persons) used and the amount they are paid.

Item 19: Financial Performance Representations: The franchisor can (but is not required to) provide information on unit financial performance.

Item 20: Outlets and Franchisee Information: Locations and contact information of existing franchises.

Item 21: Financial Statements: This section includes audited financial statements for the past three years.

Item 22: Contracts: This item includes a list of all contracts that a franchisee must sign with the franchisor. The contracts are then attached as an exhibit. These include a sample of the franchisor's standard franchise agreement and any related agreements such as a development agreement, site selection agreement, or release agreement.

Item 23: Receipts. The Franchisor must include two copies of the receipt page. This must be signed by the franchisee to confirm receipt of the document. This begins the 14-day review period. Please note, you are NOT obligated to anything by signing the receipt page, you are simply acknowledging the date the FDD was disclosed to you.

About the author

Teri O'Donnell is an entrepreneur, wife, and mom of 3 amazing and thriving young adults.

After high school, Teri took the traditional path of attending college and studied business at Illinois State University.

She's always had a sense of adventure and never wanted to live her life with regrets. This mindset is what drove Teri to the Marine Corps.

An untraditional path for a girl from the Northwest suburbs of Chicago is military. People told her not to go, especially the Marines...so she did.

After transitioning from the Marine Corps, Teri's next career path took her to a two-decade career in banking where she helped people find funding to purchase homes.

This is also when Teri discovered franchising which provided a path to financial freedom and flexibility so Teri could leave her corporate career and focus on raising her family while building their business.

People told Teri investing in a business is a big risk....so she did.

She did her due diligence, researched, drafted a business plan, and spoke with many people making sure to stay away from the naysayers. Teri had faith in her leadership abilities and the ability to create a great culture in their business.

As an investor in her 4th and 5th franchise brands, part of her purpose in life as Founder Prosperity Franchise Group, is to provide coaching and mentoring to Veterans, investors, Military spouses, and female entrepreneurs.

Whether it's investing in a franchise or turning their existing business into a franchise brand, Teri operates with the core values of what really matters in life: people, integrity, relationships, collaboration.

Believe in yourself and go for it!

If after reading this book, and you would like to know more about possible franchise opportunities, email us for a **FREE report** on the **Top 20 Franchises of the Year.**

Email:
TeriODonnell@ProsperityFranchiseGroup.com

www.ingramcontent.com/pod-product-compliance
Lightning Source LLC
Chambersburg PA
CBHW071445210326
41597CB00020B/3945